The first Stone Age people

The Stone Age was the longest period of time in human history. It began with the first people, several million years ago. These first people lived in a completely wild land. Just like all other animals, they found food from trees, roots, leaves, nuts and berries. They also caught other animals to eat.

But Stone Age people were different to other animals: they planned what to do and they made the first simple stone tools. By the end of the Stone Age they had made great **civilisations** like the ancient Egyptians.

Did you know… ?

- The first 'people' developed in East Africa, then gradually wandered in all directions until all the continents had people in.
- Stone Age people are the **ancestors** of all of us. This means we are all related to one another.
- They used sharp stones for cutting, but also blunt stones for hitting, much as we would use a hammer today.
- Stone Age people did not use money. They traded in goods. So, for example, they might trade a sharp stone for a **hide**.

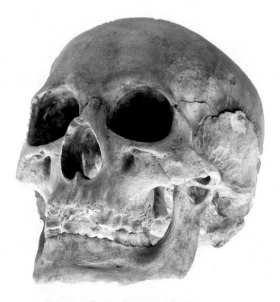

A skull of modern man

The skull of Neanderthal man

There were at least two different kinds of people in the early Stone Age world. One kind had a big forehead. They are called **Neanderthals**. The others were like us. Gradually the Neanderthals died out. We know all this from finding ancient skulls.

 Which Stone Age people died out?

3

The woolly mammoth was a creature of cold conditions (just as polar bears are today). It was hard for Stone Age people to kill because they only had spears. Usually they chased the animals towards a cliff, so the animals fell and were killed that way.

Did you know…?

- Fire was not invented until the middle of the Stone Age, so early Stone Age people had to eat their food raw.
- They could not store food, so they had to go looking for food every day.
- People sometimes used caves because caves are easily defended from wild animals, but they were mostly used as kinds of temples, not homes.
- They ate rough seeds from early wheat. But because they ate the outside as well, it wore their teeth away.

Early hunters

There were not many people in the world in Stone Age times. Almost all of the land was still covered in wild plants. Some of these plants could be eaten. Fruits could be eaten in summer and autumn, and leaves of some plants like nettles could be eaten all year.

In winter, Stone Age people dug roots of plants like wild carrots. They also tried to capture wild animals, and then skin them using flint blades. Most of what they caught was small – rabbits and ducks. All the same, they managed to hunt some of the large animals, such as mammoths, until there were none left.

Q Do you think spears could have killed mammoths?

Making flints

Sharp cutting blades were vital to the Stone Age people. They used them as we might use steel knives today.

Some rocks are very glassy and brittle. When they are struck with a sharp blow they splinter into pieces. Each of those pieces has a very sharp edge – just like a piece of broken glass.

They used flints to cut the hide off of dead animals. They used them to cut into wood. They used them on spears to hunt for food. They used them against enemies.

A flint blade was made by bashing one hard stone against a big piece of flint. It was a skilled job – just like splitting diamonds today.

Did you know… ?

- Stone Age people traded things that were important to them. They traded sharp-edge stones – flints.
- We know that flint workers sat and chipped all day because we find piles of chippings near **quarries**.
- Flint stones can be as sharp as a razor blade.

A piece made to go on a wooden shaft to form an axe.

A hand axe where the stone is used as a handle.

Q **What could you have done with a hand-held flint?**

People on the move

There was a big difference between family life at the start of the Stone Age and at the end.

For much of the time people wandered around eating fruits and nuts wherever they could find them.

But as fruits were scarce in winter, early Stone Age people had to eat animals for much of the year. The easiest way of getting meat was to fish in the rivers, but they also hunted animals.

They also probably moved with the herds of grazing animals because these animals were easy to catch. We call these wandering people **nomads**, and they may well have lived in tents made of animal hides.

In the late Stone Age, people settled down and began to farm. They could now live in wood and mud houses. They got more food in a good year. But their problem was that if the crops failed they would go hungry. The late Stone Age is the first time people began to die from hunger.

As they travelled around they only carried a few important items. They would have needed some kind of axe, and they would have needed a way to make fire – some dry straw (tinder) and stones to bang together to make sparks. The sparks caught the tinder alight.

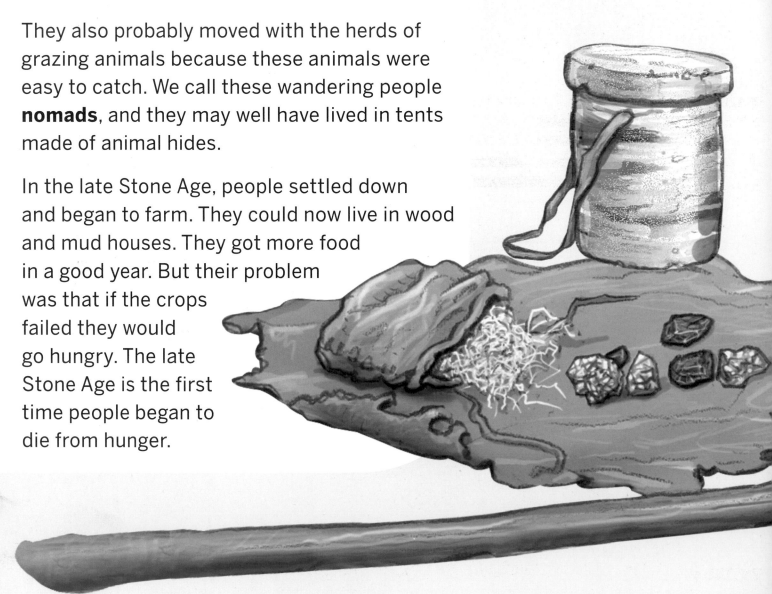

By late Stone Age times people were grinding seeds to make flour. They used a stone with a hollow in it, put a handful of grain in the hollow and rolled a round stone over the grain until it was crushed.

Did you know… ?

- Living in caves was difficult because they soon ate all the food nearby. So most early Stone Age people kept moving from place to place.
- Stone Age people lived only for twenty or thirty years because they soon got old from hard work or died from disease.
- Growing corn first started in the Middle East thousands of years before people in the west of Europe.

 When did Stone Age people die from hunger?

Cave painting

By a few tens of thousands of years ago, Stone Age people had learned to make fire for warmth and light, as well as to cook food.

Fire in a cave entrance kept wild animals out, but fire used as a light also let them paint about the world around them. This was a world full of wild animals.

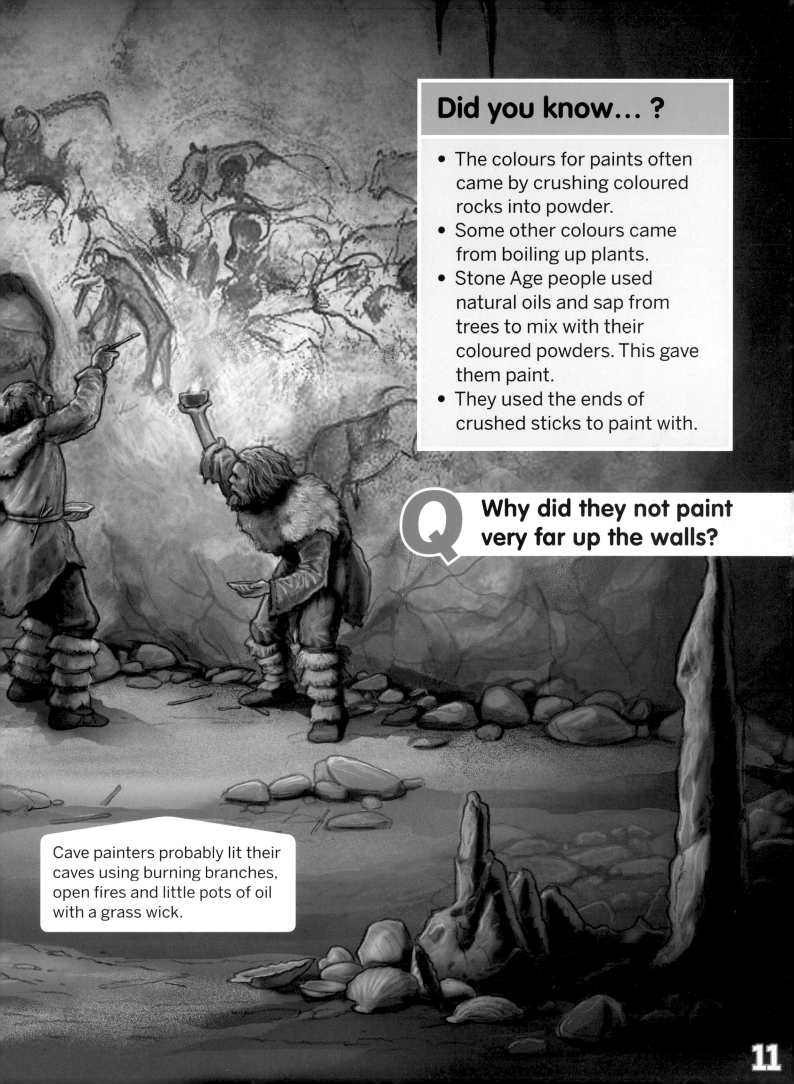

Did you know… ?

- The colours for paints often came by crushing coloured rocks into powder.
- Some other colours came from boiling up plants.
- Stone Age people used natural oils and sap from trees to mix with their coloured powders. This gave them paint.
- They used the ends of crushed sticks to paint with.

Q Why did they not paint very far up the walls?

Cave painters probably lit their caves using burning branches, open fires and little pots of oil with a grass wick.

Burying the dead

What we have seen is that Stone Age people lived in simple tents or sometimes in caves. As a result we do not find much to tell us about their lives except for their **graves**. Finding graves tells us that the Stone Age people cared about what happened to people after they died. It means they had a religion.

The earliest, and simplest, graves are made with stone slabs to make a kind of house, as you can see in this picture. The body must have been placed inside. The stone slabs were to show respect to the body, much as we use coffins today.

Did you know… ?

- Graves are found on hilltops and mountains. The Stone Age people probably thought these were the closest places to their gods.
- The stone slabs we see today were once covered with a mound of soil. We call graves above the ground 'tombs'.
- Grave slabs were very heavy and large numbers of people were needed to move each slab.
- They left no clues of how they managed to get the flat slabs on top of the upright ones because they had not learned to write, and so have not written down what they did.

Q What was a chief's grave like?

Only important people were buried this way. They were probably chiefs or priests. We do not know what happened to the others.

Barrows

As time went on, Stone Age people built enormous burial chambers. They are called long barrows.

These big graves tell us that people worshipped many gods, and had ceremonies to help the dead move into the afterlife. They tell us that ancestors were important, and needed to be treated with respect.

But we only find graves for a few people, so we know that it was probably only the rich and powerful who were buried this way.

A few painted and carved rocks still survive. This is what they look like.

Many long burial graves were marked with small stones around their edges and large stones at their head. Most of the grave is simply soil, with just a small chamber inside and a passageway leading to it.

Did you know... ?

- Only the bones were buried in barrows. The dead people were first left in the open to be picked clean by animals.
- The stones marking the graves were painted with **whorls** and curvy lines.
- The area behind the large stones was sacred and belonged to the dead. Only priests could go there.

 Who was buried in these graves?

Worship

Stone Age people in some parts of the world built great temples of large stones made into rings. Around the rings of stones were ditches and banks. They were places where people gathered each year. Temples like this are called **henges.**

There must have been huge amounts of co-operation to build these henges, but we know very little about how they organised the building of them, why they built them in circles, or how they worshipped.

What the henge at Avebury, Wiltshire may have been like during a ceremony.

Did you know… ?

- Many Stone Age peoples built pyramids to reach closer to the heavens.
- The pyramids of Egypt were built at about the same time as Stonehenge.
- Places like Stonehenge were built and rebuilt many times over many hundreds of years.
- All religious stones were probably painted, although the paint has long since gone.

Q What was built at about the same time as Stonehenge?

Famous stone circles

Britain has many famous rings of stone from Stone Age times. The most famous include Stonehenge, in southern England, and the Ring of Brodgar, on the Orkneys. The fact that there are stone circles all over the country tells us that Stone Age people were already living all over the countryside in big enough numbers to put up these great monuments.

Some stone circles have several sets of upright slabs, some have ditches, but the stones are always placed in a circle.

Brodgar, Isles of Orkney

Did you know… ?

- Building these stone circles needed hundreds or thousands of people.
- Most Stone Age people wandered over the countryside in search of food, so they had to know when to come together.
- The times that are easiest for people to know are when the Sun is highest or lowest in the sky (midsummer's day or midwinter's day).
- No one agrees on whether sunrise or sunset was important to the builders of stone circles.

Q What do all these circles have in common?

Stonehenge as seen at different times of the day.

Late Stone Age farming

By the late part of the Stone Age, say 7,000 years ago, there were far too many people to find all the food they needed in the wild.

This was the time people learned how to use wild seeds and grow them to make food crops such as wheat and barley. They also learned how to make wild animals tame and so keep them on small farms.

But the time of the Stone Age was coming to an end. People would soon learn how to use metals. This next time is called the **Bronze Age**.

Did you know… ?

- The first wheat seeds were developed in the Middle East, perhaps 10,000 years ago.
- They probably reached Europe by being traded from village to village. This was a slow process, so people in Europe only started growing wheat thousands of years after people in the Middle East.
- They probably cleared patches of ground using fire.
- They used bones tied to sticks as hoes to dig the ground and as dibbers to make holes to plant seeds.
- They had learned how to make houses to live in. Most houses were grouped together into little villages.

Patch of forest land cleared by burning to make a farmstead

Places to keep animals

Baskets

Chopped and partly burned tree trunks from the cleared forest

This smallholding is part of a group of little patches of cleared land. It made sense for people to live close together for protection from wild animals and from attack from other **tribes**.

Q **Why did they need to start farming?**

Until ploughs were introduced from Europe people used this combination of stone and wood 'chop down and pull' hoe

Simple family building

The whole family helped in farming

Birch bark bag with flint and other material to make a fire

Animal skin clothing with tendon string and bone pins

A dibber for planting seeds

Leather sandals

Hoe

This is a Stone Age house, with walls of stone and a roof of branches and reeds or turf. It had places to put a fire, stone beds and a place to store things.

The Atlantic Ocean with its winter gales and storms

Roof supports of driftwood, whalebones, etc...

'Dresser' (possibly a place for the ashes of ancestors)

Shelf

Bed

Hearth

Quern

Stone Age villages

Some of the most extraordinary remains of Stone Age times are the small houses that make a village on the Island of Orkney, Scotland. The village is called Skara Brae.

They have lasted down the centuries because they were made of stone. These were built by people who had settled down to farm in one place, and who had thought about how to keep warm and safe through the winter cold and storms.

Q Why were the houses half buried in the soil?

The lower parts of the walls were buried in soil to help keep out the wind

Low level passageways hidden from strong winds

Did you know...?

- The remains of Stone Age villages can be found from the tip of Cornwall to the top of Scotland.
- We only know about the ones made of stone because the ones made of wood have rotted away.
- No one knows why these little villages were abandoned when they seem so well-made.
- Skara Brae was buried by beach sands for four thousand years and only rediscovered in 1850.
- There are remains of sheep and cattle bones, wheat and barley seeds near the houses, telling us that they kept animals and dug the land.
- Limpet shells found nearby tell us they were also fond of seafood.

Glossary

ancestor
A relative who lived a long time ago.

Bronze Age
The time after the Stone Age when people started using bronze metal.

civilisation
A group of people who used writing and lived in towns and cities.

grave
The place where the body of a person is buried.

henge
A circle made of standing stones, a ditch and a bank.

hide
The skin of a dead animal. It is often used to make things like clothes.

Neanderthal
A variety of people who lived in the early Stone Age. They had large foreheads.

nomad
Somebody who moves around looking for food, instead of living in one place.

quarry
A place where people dig for stone.

tribe
A group of related people living and working together.

whorl
A spiral or curl pattern used as decoration.

Index

Curriculum Visions

Curriculum Visions Explorers
This series provides straightforward introductions to key worlds and ideas.

You might also be interested in
Our slightly more detailed book, The Stone Age, and others such as Exploring the first civilisations, Celtic times, The ancient Egyptians, The ancient Greeks, The Romans in Britain and Exploring ancient Rome.

www.CurriculumVisions.com

(Subscription required)

© Atlantic Europe Publishing 2014

First reprint 2014. Second reprint 2014. Third reprint 2014.

The right of Brian Knapp to be identified as the author of this work has been asserted by him in accordance with the Copyright, Designs and Patents Act 1988.

Author
Brian Knapp, BSc, PhD

Senior Designer
Adele Humphries, BA, PGCE

Editors
Gillian Gatehouse
Emily Pulsford, BA

Illustrations
Mark Stacey, except p19 David Woodroffe

Designed and produced by
Atlantic Europe Publishing

Printed in China by
WKT Company Ltd

Exploring life in the Stone Age – Curriculum Visions
A CIP record for this book is available from the British Library.

Paperback ISBN 978 1 78278 075 5

Picture credits
All photographs are from the Earthscape and ShutterStock Picture Libraries.

This product is manufactured from sustainable managed forests. For every tree cut down at least one more is planted.